WHY EVERYTHING FEELS OFF FINANCIALLY

How Government Policy, Global Conflict, and Hidden Financial System Pressures Are Reshaping Your Money

By André J. Porter

Quiet Mechanics Press

WHY EVERYTHING FEELS OFF FINANCIALLY

Printed in the United States of America.

Published by Quiet Mechanics Press.

DISCLAIMER

This manuscript is for informational and educational purposes only. It does not constitute financial, legal, tax, or investment advice, and no professional relationship is created by this material.

This book is built around observable policy actions, public events, legal developments, financial-market behavior, and the effects those things appear to be having on ordinary life. Its purpose is not to claim access to hidden knowledge. Its purpose is to explain a pattern clearly enough that the reader can decide whether it matches what they are still living through.

References to specific assets, networks, or financial instruments are illustrative only and are not recommendations to buy, sell, or hold any security, token, or other financial product.

For those trying to make sense of a financial system that no longer makes sense.

CONTENTS

INTRODUCTION

Everything Feels Off — And Why That Matters

Something in daily life feels wrong. Not catastrophic. Not collapsing. Just tighter, heavier, and harder to explain. People feel it in groceries, in housing, in insurance, in the way work feels less stable and money stretches less far.

The strange part is that none of this aligns with the signals people were taught to watch. Financial markets still function. Banks still operate. The government and financial system haven't snapped. Headlines swing between optimism and concern, but nothing delivers the clean reset people keep expecting.

Before going further, one idea needs to be made plain. This book uses the word "system" in a specific way. The "government system" refers to the institutions that tax, spend, regulate, and stabilize. The "financial system" refers to the banks, markets, lenders, and intermediaries that move money and absorb risk. Most of the pressure in this story comes from the interaction between the two — the combined government and financial system — because neither side can function without the other. When this book says "the system," it means the structure created when government incentives and financial incentives lock together.

It shows how pressure moved step by step through labor, trade, food, energy, confidence, and finally the financial system itself. It shows how the government rebuilt the plumbing beneath money when policy alone couldn't restore the old baseline. And it shows how the squeeze shows up in cash, bonds, metals, and daily life.

Most importantly, it gives the reader a way to understand the environment without waiting for someone else to explain it. Once the pattern becomes visible, the contradiction disappears. Life feels tight because the burden has been moved — not removed.

The story isn't over. It is unfolding.

That is where this book has to begin, because that is where most people already are. They feel it before they ever have a name for it. They feel it when groceries still cost too much, when insurance rises again, when housing does not reset, when repairs cost more than expected, and when even a bigger paycheck does not create the breathing room it used to.

At the same time, financial markets are still functioning. That is what makes the moment so disorienting. If life is this tight, why are financial markets not breaking in the same way? If the burden is this real, why is it showing up as a long squeeze rather than one obvious collapse? If things are supposed to be "stable," why do the parts of life people actually have to pay for still feel unstable?

That contradiction is not imagined. It is structural.

When this book says government, it does not mean one office, one president, or one agency acting alone. It means the larger machine made up of executive orders, agency enforcement, courts, central banking, trade policy, energy policy, and the financial markets where money is invested and priced. It means the network of decisions and institutions that determines how pressure moves.

When this book says purchasing power, it means what money can actually buy. If food, housing, insurance, and transport rise faster than a paycheck, then purchasing power is falling even if the number on the paycheck is higher.

And when this book says financial repression, it means something that sounds technical but is easier to understand than it first appears. Financial repression is what happens when the government system has a debt and stability problem it cannot solve cleanly, and instead of forcing one large, visible reset, it allows the burden to move slowly into everyday life. In plain English, the structure keeps functioning while money buys less, essential costs stay high, and ordinary people keep adjusting.

Repression rarely arrives as force. It arrives as environment. The government does not need to compel participation. It only needs to create conditions where most people respond in predictable ways. They hold cash because uncertainty makes that feel safe. They delay decisions because they still expect things to normalize. They wait for prices to come back down. While they wait, the system keeps moving.

That is the story this book tells.

It begins with the problem the government could not solve honestly. It then moves through immigration enforcement, labor disruption, tariffs, trade friction, food and housing pressure, energy shocks, legal changes, financial-market support, technological substitution, and global repositioning. It explains how those actions pushed the country through recognizable stages of repression. And it shows how ordinary people, without meaning to, were drawn into the transfer itself.

The point is not to predict a single dramatic ending. The point is to make the pattern readable. Because once the pattern becomes visible, what felt disconnected begins to feel connected.

WHAT THIS BOOK IS REALLY ABOUT

This is not a textbook and it is not a trading manual. It is a story about how the government system, under pressure, kept choosing continuity over honesty, stability over reset, and gradual loss over one visible reckoning.

The book is not arguing that one hidden meeting produced a perfect script for everything that followed. It is arguing something more practical: a series of deliberate policy choices, legal actions, enforcement shifts, and institutional responses produced outcomes that kept moving in the same direction. They protected financial-market function. They made the debt burden easier to carry in real terms. And they shifted more of the adjustment into the parts of life ordinary people cannot avoid.

That is what financial repression means in this book. It is not a slogan. It is the name for the pattern that appears when the government system refuses a clean reset and instead spreads the burden across time.

To understand that pattern, one more phrase needs to be made simple: financial rails. Financial rails are the hidden pathways money uses to move — direct deposits, bank transfers, debit-card transactions, and institutional settlements. Most people never think about those rails because they only see the money arrive. But once the government system comes under pressure, the question of how money moves — how fast, how cheaply, how clearly, and under whose rules — starts to matter a lot more.

That is why infrastructure, payment systems, settlement, and digital rails all belong later in this story.

There is one more point that has to be made clearly before the timeline begins. When someone holds cash while prices keep rising, it feels safe in the short run because cash is simple and immediate. But over time, the purchasing power inside that cash keeps shrinking. The number stays the same. Life gets more expensive around it.

That lost purchasing power does not simply disappear. Part of it shows up in higher prices. Part of it shows up in assets that reprice faster than cash. And part of it makes the government system's debt easier to carry, because debt fixed in dollars becomes less burdensome when those dollars buy less in real life.

That is one of the hidden mechanics of repression.

And it does not stop inside the United States. Countries around the world hold Treasury notes and bonds. Central banks hold them. Sovereign wealth funds hold them. Pension systems hold them. Insurance companies hold them. The dollar system allows the U.S. government to borrow from the rest of the world and still remain at the center of global finance. That means when the government system keeps paying nominally while the dollars it pays back are losing real purchasing power, the adjustment is not only domestic.

It spreads globally.

That is why this book is not just about what happened inside the United States. It is also about what the rest of the world still has to absorb when the dollar-centered system chooses continuity over clarity.

That is the story.

PART I

THE PROBLEM THEY COULDN'T SOLVE

Why the government never reset, and why the burden had to move somewhere.

CHAPTER 1

The Debt Problem Is Still Here

How an unresolved debt burden quietly shapes everything else.

Every government in modern history that has carried too much debt has eventually faced the same three options: grow out of it, default on it, or cut spending sharply enough to force a reset. Each option works on paper. None of them are politically survivable today.

Growth is not strong enough. Default would tear through a financial system where almost every institution holds the same Treasury debt as collateral. Austerity would create the very recession the government is trying to avoid. So the United States is doing the only thing left — carrying the debt forward and letting time, inflation, and the real economy do the adjusting.

That choice is the starting point of everything in this book. The debt has not been paid down. It has not been restructured. It has not been forgiven. It is being carried. And because it is being carried, the burden of carrying it has to land somewhere. It lands in food, in housing, in insurance, in the narrowing of household flexibility — in the parts of life ordinary people cannot avoid.

This is what it looks like when the debt problem is unresolved but the government refuses a clean reset. The burden does not disappear. It changes location.

CHAPTER 2

Why It Still Hasn't Broken All at Once

Why the financial system spreads losses instead of revealing them.

If the debt burden is this real, the next question is obvious:

Why hasn't the financial system broken? Why haven't financial markets collapsed in a way that matches the financial pressure people feel in daily life? Why hasn't there been one clean reset that forces the truth into the open? Because the government is still trying to avoid exactly that.

A visible break would force recognition. It would force losses into view. It would make the debt problem impossible to describe as temporary. But a financially-pressured government and financial system don't need everything to improve. They only need enough of the structure to keep functioning. That's the difference between -- a reset, which concentrates the pain, and repression, which spreads it. This is why the environment feels so strange. Nothing snaps cleanly. Instead, the burden moves through - food, housing, insurance, and work, while financial markets remain supported enough to avoid panic.

There are two kinds of loss -- Visible loss: a company fails, a market crashes and everyone sees it; and quiet loss: the grocery bill stays high, insurance rises again, and housing never returns to where it was. Cash keeps the same number but buys less life. The first kind gets headlines. The second kind gets normalized. The government keeps choosing the second path. Not because it's painless — but because it's survivable. The burden hasn't vanished. It has been redistributed.

PART II

THE TIMELINE

How financial pressure moved through labor, trade, food, energy, and confidence.

CHAPTER 3

Immigration, Enforcement, and the First Pressure Shift

How labor disruption became the first transmission channel.

The first major financial pressure shift didn't begin in financial markets. It began in labor.

When the administration returned to office, one of its earliest priorities was immigration enforcement. On January 20, 2025, the White House issued an executive order titled "Protecting the American People Against Invasion," revoking earlier directives and signaling a more aggressive posture.

This was followed by:

- a broad asylum ban;
- a border emergency declaration;
- troop deployments to the southern border
- new ICE initiatives, including a 2026 "Birth Tourism Initiative".

Large parts of the U.S. economy depend on labor that is highly sensitive to immigration policy especially agriculture, construction, and labor-intensive services. These sectors didn't need a dramatic collapse to feel the effect. They only needed less predictability. That's what happened.

As enforcement became more visible — workplace checks, detentions, removals — behavior changed:

- some workers avoided certain jobs or locations;
- some became less willing to move between employers; and
- some became harder to hire or retain.

Employers didn't face "no labor." They faced weaker reliability. And when timing matters — crops, construction, logistics — weaker reliability becomes cost. Farmers paid more to secure labor. Contractors built more delay into timelines. Businesses raised prices to protect margins. Those costs didn't stay with them. They moved outward — into food, housing, and services. This was the first stage of repression shifting into the second. Financial markets still looked stable.

But daily life began tightening in ways people could feel before they could explain. A deeper blueprint was also at work. Reuters reported that Trump brought several Project 2025–aligned figures into the administration, keeping its emphasis on stronger executive control and faster implementation alive in practice.

The average household didn't need to know any of this.

They felt it in:

- the grocery bill;
- the housing search; and
- the sense that costs were rising in places no one was describing honestly.

That's how financial pressure began.

CHAPTER 4

Tariffs, Neighbors, and How Cost Started Spreading Faster

Why trade friction pushed prices higher and kept them there.

Once labor shifted, trade spread the financial pressure faster. Tariffs sound distant, but they work simply:

- the importer pays more first;
- then the distributor;
- then the retailer;
- and then the household.

In March 2025, Trump locked in 25% tariffs on most goods from Mexico and Canada. Reuters reported that the move pushed North America toward a regional trade war and sent markets reeling. Canada responded with retaliatory tariffs on nearly $30 billion of U.S. goods.

This mattered because North America's supply chains are deeply integrated. Parts, materials, agricultural products, and manufacturing inputs move constantly across borders.

When friction increases, movement becomes less smooth, costs rise, and the old baseline disappears.

A builder paying more for materials doesn't need a headline to know something changed. A grocer facing higher transport costs doesn't need a speech to know prices aren't coming back down.

A manufacturer relying on cross-border components doesn't need ideology to understand that friction has become cost.

Prices didn't need to keep exploding. They only needed to reset higher and stay there long enough for people to stop expecting a return to the old level. That's what began happening. And because it kept happening, people began to change their behavior. (On February 20, 2026, the U.S. Supreme Court ruled that the legal basis for most of these tariffs was invalid, leaving the trade picture more uncertain rather than less.)

CHAPTER 5

Farms, Meat, Vegetables, Fertilizer, and the Grocery Bill

How food became the most personal form of financial pressure.

Food is where the story stops sounding abstract. A farm doesn't produce "inflation."

It produces vegetables, fruit, grain, feed, and livestock. Each depends on labor, energy, fertilizer, water, transport, and timing. Once labor became less reliable and trade friction raised input costs, agriculture began carrying financial pressure from multiple directions at once.

Fertilizer is the clearest example. Most people never think about it until food prices rise. But fertilizer determines what it costs to grow crops at scale. If fertilizer rises, farming rises. If fuel rises, farming rises again. If transport rises, the final price rises again.

Meat follows the same logic -- livestock depends on feed, feed depends on grain, grain depends on fertilizer, energy, and logistics.

Vegetables feel pressure differently -- timing matters more, labor matters more, and spoilage matters more.

If labor is less reliable, fertilizer is more expensive, and transport still costs more, produce remains expensive even without a catastrophic shortage. That's why the grocery bill matters so much in this book. It's not just annoying. It's the place where the second stage of repression becomes personal. The household doesn't need a chart. They only need to look at the total and realize the old baseline hasn't returned.

Food is one of the most important transmission channels in the story.

The government system doesn't need to announce that people are being squeezed. It only needs to create conditions where food stays expensive long enough for life to reorganize around it.

CHAPTER 6

AI, Robotics, Layoffs, and the New Labor Math

Why businesses adapted structurally—and why households felt it.

Once labor became harder to rely on and trade raised input costs, businesses began changing how they operated.

At first, the response was predictable -- pay more where necessary, delay where possible, pass along cost when customers could absorb it. But eventually the question changed. It stopped being: "How do we survive higher cost?" It became: "How do we depend less on the parts of the financial system that have become unstable?" That's where automation, robotics, and AI shifted from future strategy to immediate cost response. If labor is more expensive, more fragile, and more politically exposed, then replacing part of it with software, machines, or AI-supported workflows stops looking optional.

Reuters reported -- companies were still cutting jobs while increasing AI investment, the federal workforce shrank by ~12% between late 2024 and early 2026, and SEC headcount fell 18% under Trump. This changed the texture of the economy. Now the government system wasn't just imposing higher cost. It was weakening income certainty at the same time.

Households can survive rising prices if they trust future work. They can survive unstable work if life is getting cheaper. But when higher cost and weaker job security arrive together, behavior changes faster. People hold more cash, delay more decisions, narrow their lives sooner. This is one of the clearest signs that the third stage of repression is beginning. The issue is no longer just price. It's adaptation.

CHAPTER 7

Energy, Iran, the Strait of Hormuz, Desalination, Venezuela

How global energy pressure accelerated domestic cost.

Labor shifted the financial system. Trade spread the financial pressure. Energy accelerated it. Energy sits underneath almost every cost system, including transportation, fertilizer, farming, construction materials, shipping, and insurance.

In parts of the Middle East, it also sits under water, because desalination depends heavily on energy. That's why the war around Iran and the disruption tied to the Strait of Hormuz matter so much.

Reuters reported:

- flows through one of the world's most critical energy corridors were disrupted;
- the U.S. military was enforcing a blockade tied to Iranian ports; and
- ships were being turned back.

Oil doesn't need to disappear for the financial system to feel pressure. It only needs to become uncertain. Uncertainty raises shipping costs, insurance costs, and expected prices of moving oil and gas.

That financial pressure moves into fertilizer. Fertilizer is energy-intensive, especially when natural gas is involved. Reuters reported fertilizer shortages as a major concern linked to the Iran war because transport and energy pressure threatened global planting cycles. Once fertilizer stays expensive, farms pay more. Once farms pay more, food carries the financial pressure forward. Water pressure matters too. Desalination is essential in the Gulf. When energy is expensive, water is expensive. When water is expensive, food and household costs rise.

The IMF cut growth forecasts for the Middle East and North Africa. Gulf exporters faced financial pressure from disrupted output, shipping, and confidence. Support for U.S. policy becomes more conditional when domestic strain rises.

There's also a physical issue most Americans never think about - not all oil is interchangeable. The U.S. produces a lot of light crude. But many U.S. refineries were built to process heavy crude more efficiently. That's why Venezuela matters. Reuters reported that Gulf Coast refineries were prepared to run Venezuelan heavy crude and still have a practical appetite for it. This wasn't just diplomacy. It was about keeping the refining system efficient while Middle Eastern heavy supply was under pressure.

This moved the financial system more fully into the third stage of repression. The burden was no longer just labor or trade. It was labor, trade, energy, plus global alignment pressure all at once. (By March 2026 the situation had escalated sharply: Iran declared the Strait of Hormuz closed, Brent crude briefly surged past $120 per barrel, and the International Energy Agency described the disruption as the largest supply shock in the history of the global oil market.)

CHAPTER 8

Citizenship, Voting Rights, Race, Leadership Behavior, Confidence

Why trust, belonging, and stability matter economically.

By this point, it's no longer enough to talk only about prices. The government is also moving through confidence, trust, and belonging. Citizenship policy matters because it changes how people feel inside the rules. Trump's push to limit birthright citizenship is still not settled. Reuters reported in April 2026 that the Supreme Court remained skeptical of key parts of the effort.

At the same time, proof-of-citizenship voting restrictions tied to Trump-backed initiatives were spreading through states — with similar rules active or developing in 23 states.

Legal belonging changes behavior before it changes law. If people feel less certain about their status, their rights, and their recognition, they move more cautiously.

Employers become less certain about labor continuity. Communities become less secure. Confidence thins. There is also a racial undertone that cannot be softened. The administration's attacks on DEI, its rhetoric about fighting "anti-white feeling," and the clustering of immigration, citizenship, and voting-rights pressure changed how many people read the direction of the government system. Reuters reported on Trump's pledge to fight what he called an "anti-white feeling" and on efforts to dismantle DEI structures in government and pressure the private sector. Critics argued these moves rolled back civil-rights protections and changed who felt fully included.

Perception matters. Financial systems run on trust as much as money. Leadership behavior adds another layer. When a leader is widely perceived as erratic or volatile, institutions become more cautious. Allies become more conditional. Markets carry another layer of uncertainty.

The third stage of repression is not just economic. It is institutional and psychological.

CHAPTER 9

The Federal Reserve, Liquidity, and Why Markets Still Hold

How liquidity supports markets even while life tightens.

At this point, the reader's question becomes unavoidable -- If all of this is happening, why are financial markets still holding? The answer begins with liquidity — how easy it is to get and use money right now. As long as enough money is still moving, financial markets can remain supported even while daily life tightens.

The Federal Reserve is trapped between two risks:

- tighten too much → damage markets and the broader economy; and
- ease too quickly → worsen embedded inflation in food, energy, housing, and insurance.

So, it balances. And while it balances, liquidity supports financial markets. This doesn't mean the financial system is healthy. It means the government system is still choosing where the burden appears first. So far, it is choosing ordinary life before a full financial-market rupture. That's why the contradiction persists. Markets hold. Life tightens. The burden continues moving elsewhere.

PART III

HOW THE GOVERNMENT SYSTEM CHANGED ITSELF

When policy wasn't enough, the government system rebuilt its plumbing.

CHAPTER 10

Financial Rails, Settlement, and the Hidden Rebuild

Why the financial system began upgrading the pipes beneath money.

Once the government system realized the old baseline wasn't coming back, it shifted from managing financial pressure to rebuilding infrastructure. Most people never think about how money moves. But every paycheck, every debit-card swipe, every bank transfer, every international settlement — all of it moves through hidden pathways. Those pathways are financial rails. When a financial system becomes constrained, the qualities of those rails matter more than speed, clarity, cost, control, and finality.

This is where settlement becomes important. Settlement is the moment a payment is final -- the difference between the payment being initiated and the money arriving. Faster settlement means less delay, less capital tied up waiting, and fewer points of failure. In a financial pressured government system, that matters because the government system needs money to move efficiently, it needs fewer bottlenecks, and it needs more control over the rails themselves. This is why infrastructure belongs in the story. It's not a side note. It's what a pressured system does when it stops expecting a clean return to the old world.

The rebuild is quiet.

But it is real.

CHAPTER 11

Crypto, Utility, and Whether New Rails Can Help the U.S.

Why digital settlement matters more than speculation.

Crypto enters the story here — but not for the reasons most people think. Crypto has two different stories: Speculation -- prices rise and fall with excitement, momentum, and easy money; and Utility -- financial systems that move value faster, cheaper, or with less friction.

This book cares about the second story.

Several categories of digital networks are built around movement rather than hype. The examples below are illustrative, not recommendations. They are listed only to show what utility-focused infrastructure looks like in practice.

- Payment and cross-border settlement networks — designed to move value quickly with low cost. Examples include XRP (Ripple), XLM (Stellar), and Algorand (ALGO).
- Enterprise and trade-finance rails — designed to interoperate with existing institutional systems. Examples include XDC Network and Hedera (HBAR).
- Programmable smart-contract platforms — designed to automate agreements and tokenize assets. Examples include Ethereum (ETH), Avalanche (AVAX), and Solana (SOL).
- Stablecoins — dollar-denominated digital tokens used for settlement and remittance. Examples include USDC, USDT, and PYUSD.
- Central-bank digital-currency frameworks — government-issued digital money already in pilot or live use. Examples include China's e-CNY, the European Central Bank's digital

euro work, and the Bank for International Settlements' cross-border experiments.

Each category carries different risks, regulatory profiles, and design tradeoffs. None of them are endorsements. They appear here because each one illustrates a different way digital rails are being built and tested in real systems. If the U.S. integrates useful digital financial rails, it may strengthen the dollar system by making it faster and more efficient. If it pushes those digital systems away or leaves them in regulatory limbo, it may encourage alternatives outside its control. Reuters reported that Trump ordered a crypto working group in January 2025 and continued pressing for a more accommodating legal structure for digital assets and stablecoins.

This doesn't settle the debate. But it shows that crypto policy is no longer a sideshow. It is part of the financial system question. Crypto belongs in this book not because price action is exciting, but because financial rails matter more than most people realize.

CHAPTER 12

The Legal Shift That Changed the Incentives

How legal discretion, enforcement, and incentives reshaped the landscape.

The most important changes in a financially-pressured government system rarely begin with brand-new laws. They begin with new readings of existing laws, new enforcement priorities, and new incentives that change how institutions behave. That is what happened as the debt burden grew too large to resolve cleanly. The government system did not announce a dramatic legal overhaul. It changed the legal environment inside the machinery it already had.

The first shift was interpretive. Agencies gained broader room to define what counted as compliance, what counted as risk, and what counted as a violation. Courts, facing political pressure and rising caseloads, often gave agencies more room to act. That mattered because it let the government system move faster without waiting for Congress to build an entirely new framework.

The second shift was enforcement. Penalties increased. Investigations accelerated. The threshold for intervention dropped. Businesses, lenders, insurers, and service providers found themselves operating under a more assertive regulatory posture. The message was simple: instability would not be allowed to spread into financial markets if the government system could contain it somewhere else.

The third shift was incentive-based. Once the direction of enforcement became clear, institutions began adapting before they were forced to. Compliance departments expanded. Legal teams grew more cautious. Risk officers became more conservative. The system did not need to command behavior directly. It only needed to make the cost of noncompliance feel higher than the cost of adjustment.

That change in incentives mattered because it produced predictability, even while life felt less flexible. Predictability supported markets. Markets supported confidence. Confidence supported the appearance of stability. And stability allowed the debt burden to be carried forward without a visible reset.

Most people never saw the legal shift as a legal shift. They felt it in stricter rules, in faster penalties, in narrower approvals, in tougher claims processes, and in the growing complexity of ordinary transactions. They felt the system becoming less forgiving even when no one could point to one dramatic new law.

This was not a hidden conspiracy. It was a structural adaptation. A government system under pressure used interpretation, enforcement, and incentives because they were faster than legislation and cheaper than reform. The legal shift did not solve the problem. It made the problem more manageable and changed how everyone inside the system responded to pressure.

That is why this chapter matters. Before the government system could rebuild capacity, it first had to reshape the rules, expectations, and consequences inside which that capacity would operate. The legal shift set the terms. The quieter operational rebuild came next.

CHAPTER 13

The Quiet Rebuild of Government Capacity

Why agencies, regulators, and government machinery adapted faster than the public realized.

The next change was less visible but just as important. Once the legal environment became more flexible for agencies and less forgiving for everyone else, the government system still needed the practical ability to act on that advantage. It needed more capacity, better coordination, and faster execution.

That is what happened in the years after the debt problem became too large to solve cleanly. The government system did not announce a grand redesign. It rebuilt itself quietly -- through systems, staffing priorities, administrative coordination, and speed.

The first shift was operational. Agencies modernized internal systems, improved data handling, and reduced delays in how cases, payments, oversight, and enforcement moved through the bureaucracy. A government system under pressure does not only want authority. It wants throughput.

The second shift was coordination. Immigration enforcement, financial oversight, energy regulation, trade compliance, and related parts of government became easier to connect in practice. Information moved faster across departments. And when information moves faster, pressure can be redirected faster too.

The third shift was execution. Once agencies had better systems and clearer signals, decisions could be made sooner, actions could be sequenced more tightly, and responses could be carried out with less drift. The public often experiences that as sudden rigidity. Internally, it looks like a machine learning to move with fewer wasted motions.

This is where capacity becomes different from law. Law defines the room to act. Capacity determines how much can actually be done inside that room. The government system did not become more transparent. It became more capable.

That quiet rebuild mattered because it allowed the system to stabilize markets, redirect flows, and enforce new norms without staging one large visible overhaul. It allowed repression to work through administration, coordination, and execution rather than through headline-level force.

Most people never saw the rebuild itself. They felt it in the speed of decisions, in the rigidity of processes, in the way explanations arrived after actions, and in the sense that institutions had become harder to slow down once they started moving.

Capacity became a tool of continuity. Continuity became a substitute for clarity. And the system became better at managing pressure than acknowledging it. This was not the end of the story. It was the infrastructure for everything that followed.

PART IV

WHAT HAPPENS TO YOUR MONEY

How the squeeze shows up in cash, bonds, gold, and real life.

CHAPTER 14

Cash, Purchasing Power, and the Quiet Loss

Why cash feels safe but loses purchasing power.

Cash feels safe because it is immediate. If someone needs money today, cash works. It doesn't require a market to open. It doesn't need to be sold. It doesn't depend on anyone else's decision. That's why households trust it when life becomes uncertain. But under a stage of repression, cash becomes a place where value (and thus purchasing power) can quietly disappear.

Imagine someone keeps ten thousand dollars in cash because they're worried about what comes next. The number doesn't change. It still says ten thousand. But if food keeps rising, housing stays elevated, insurance climbs again, and repairs cost more, then that same ten thousand buys less life than it did before. The number looks safe. The life inside it shrinks. This is purchasing power in real life.

Many people assume that if their bank balance is unchanged, they're preserving their position. In reality, they may be losing ground every month without seeing a single dramatic loss. That lost value doesn't vanish. It shows up in higher prices, assets that adjust faster than cash, and a government system whose debts become easier to carry when the dollars used to repay them buy less.

This is one of the hidden mechanics of repression. The government system still pays. The public still adjusts. The transfer keeps happening.

CHAPTER 15

Treasury Notes, Treasury Bonds, and the Global Burden

How the U.S. pays its debts—while shifting the real cost.

A Treasury note or bond is simply a loan to the U.S. government. When a person, pension fund, insurer, sovereign wealth fund, or foreign central bank buys one, they are lending money to the United States in exchange for interest and repayment later. It sounds safe. And in one sense, it is. The government still pays. But there is a difference between being repaid in dollars and being repaid in dollars that still buy the same amount of life.

Imagine a foreign central bank buys one hundred million dollars in Treasury notes. The United States pays the interest exactly as promised. Later, it returns the principal. There is no default. But if the dollars returned buy less food, less energy, less industrial input, and less real life than the dollars originally lent, then that lender has still absorbed part of the adjustment. This is how repression becomes global. Countries around the world hold Treasury debt and dollar reserves. They still get paid. But they can still lose in real terms if the dollars coming back are weaker than expected. The burden spreads not through default, but through diminished purchasing power inside continued payment. It is one of the least understood parts of the story — and one of the most important.

CHAPTER 16

Gold, Silver, and Why Repricing Starts There

Why metals often move before the public understands the shift.

Gold matters because it often responds early when the government system begins to look less trustworthy. Gold is not someone else's liability. It does not depend on repayment. It does not rely on a promise. That's why it becomes more relevant when the government system keeps functioning, but confidence inside it begins to thin.

Silver behaves differently. It often lags at first because it sits closer to industrial demand, manufacturing cycles, and financial-market volatility. Then it accelerates once the repricing becomes more active. This is why the sequence matters -- Gold often signals that the problem is becoming monetary; and Silver often signals that the financial market is beginning to accept that the financial pressure is not temporary. Neither moves in a straight line. In periods of panic, even gold and silver can be sold if people need immediate cash. But over time, they tend to mean more in a system where money itself is quietly losing ground.

PART V

THE STAGES OF REPRESSION

How to read where the financial system is—and where it's going.

CHAPTER 17

Crypto Between Speculation and Utility

Why movement-based systems matter in a financially-pressured environment.

Crypto stays split between two stories. One story is speculation. Prices rise and fall with excitement, momentum, and easy money. The other story is utility. Digital systems that move value faster, cheaper, or with less friction. This book cares about the second story.

In a stage of repression, systems that reduce settlement friction, move value quickly, or create new rails, become more interesting to both private actors and governments. This doesn't make them safe or guaranteed. It makes them relevant. Crypto policy is no longer a sideshow. It is part of the larger question of whether the U.S. modernizes its rails or leaves that opportunity to others.

CHAPTER 18

The First Stage of Repression

When people still expect normalization.

The first stage is easy to miss. Prices may be rising, but people still believe the financial pressure is temporary. They expect the old baseline to return. Financial markets look calm. Headlines sound manageable. Households assume patience will solve the problem. Nothing looks dramatic enough yet. This is why the first stage is so deceptive.

The financial system is already shifting — but the public still believes in the old world.

CHAPTER 19

The Second Stage of Repression

When life tightens but hope for a reset remains.

The second stage begins when the financial pressure becomes visible in daily life. Food stays high. Housing remains elevated. Insurance keeps rising. People feel the squeeze, but they still believe the financial system will reset if they wait long enough. This is managed erosion. The burden is now visible enough to hurt, but not visible enough to force a larger reckoning. People still expect relief. They still expect the old baseline to return. But it doesn't.

CHAPTER 20

The Third Stage of Repression

When behavior changes before people name the change.

The third stage is where the country appears to be now. Financial pressure has lasted long enough to change behavior, people hold cash more defensively, businesses adapt structurally, the government system redesigns parts of itself, financial markets still hold, confidence is thinner, and life is narrower. People begin living inside the new conditions before fully naming them. This is the stage where the squeeze becomes a way of life, not a temporary disruption.

CHAPTER 21

The Fourth Stage of Repression

When adaptation hardens into structure.

The fourth stage begins when adaptation becomes permanent. New rails matter more. Old assumptions matter less. The financial system begins to look stable again — but it is a narrower, more controlled stability. This is why the fourth stage can feel like recovery when it is actually lock-in. People stop waiting for the old world to return. They begin adjusting to the new one. The financial system hasn't collapsed. It has settled.

CHAPTER 22

How to Tell Which Stage Is Active

A simple checklist for reading the environment.

The easiest way to read the stage of repression is not to ask whether headlines sound calmer. It is to ask whether: food remains high; housing is still elevated; insurance keeps rising; energy is still transmitting financial pressure; financial markets are still being supported by liquidity; and people are still changing their behavior because they no longer trust the old baseline. If those things are still true, the stage of repression is still active.

This checklist gives the reader something they've never had before -- a way to understand the environment without waiting for someone else to explain it.

PART VI

WHAT COMES NEXT

Why the transfer continues—and why the contradiction persists.

CHAPTER 23

When Financial Pressure and Liquidity Keep Moving Together

Why the financial system still holds while life still tightens.

As long as cost pressure remains high and liquidity remains the main support for financial markets, the contradiction continues. The government system can keep carrying the burden as long as enough liquidity remains in the structure, enough confidence remains in the dollar, and enough of the system still functions smoothly. But every month that food stays high, housing remains elevated, energy transmits pressure, insurance keeps rising, and financial markets remain supported by liquidity, the pattern deepens.

The financial system is not resetting. It is continuing. That continuation is the story.

CHAPTER 24

The Largest Transfer of Wealth

How purchasing power moves quietly from the public to the financial system.

The largest transfer of wealth is not one moment. It is not a crash. It is not a headline. It is the ongoing process through which ordinary people lose purchasing power while the larger structure remains functional enough to avoid panic. This transfer happens because the conditions that drive it are still in place -- food is still high, housing remains elevated, insurance keeps rising, cash loses ground in real terms, financial markets are supported by liquidity, and the debt burden becomes easier to carry when the money used to repay it buys less.

The transfer does not happen dramatically. It happens persistently. That is why most people don't see it clearly. They feel it — but they don't name it.

The government doesn't force participation. It creates conditions where participation becomes the default.

CHAPTER 25

Why Everything Still Feels Off

Why the squeeze is structural, not emotional.

Everything still feels off because the debt problem remains, the burden is still being shifted, and the government is still choosing continuity over a visible reset. This is not mood. It is structure.

The point of this book is not to predict the exact ending. It is to make the pattern readable enough that the reader no longer mistakes the squeeze for randomness. Once the pattern becomes visible the contradiction disappears, the reader understands why life keeps tightening while markets still hold, and they can see where the burden is moving. The story is not over. It is unfolding.

PART VII

IF FULL REPRESSION TAKES HOLD

What a later stage looks like—and why it doesn't feel like collapse.

CHAPTER 26

If Full Repression Takes Hold

Why narrowing—not breaking—is the real risk.

If full repression takes hold, it will not arrive with a single headline. It will not look like a collapse. It will look like what people are already feeling, only more permanent. The system will still function, paychecks will still come in, financial markets will still operate, and bills will still be paid. But life will feel tighter in a way that does not go away. Food will not just feel expensive for a season. It will feel like something people plan around. Housing will not simply feel out of reach for a moment. It will remain elevated long enough that fewer people expect to catch up. Insurance will stop feeling like protection. It will feel like another cost that cannot be avoided.

Nothing will break. But nothing will loosen. That is what a later stage of repression feels like. The change is not only financial. It is behavioral. People begin adjusting in ways they do not always recognize at first they delay decisions longer, they reduce spending more quickly, and then they hold onto cash because movement feels risky.

At first, that feels responsible. Over time, it becomes limiting. Life narrows. This is where the middle-class story becomes clear. The middle class does not disappear all at once. It stretches. Households that still look stable begin living with less margin, they still work, they still pay, they still try to save, but the buffer is gone. One unexpected cost matters more. One job disruption matters more. One policy shift matters more. That is how a middle class thins. Not through a single collapse. Through financial pressure that does not release. Work changes too. Jobs still exist. But they feel less secure. People trust them less. They plan less confidently around them.

Income becomes something to protect rather than something to build from. Repression is not only about price. It is about confidence. If people stop believing that effort leads to stability, the system changes in a deeper way. It becomes defensive. And once a system becomes defensive, it becomes harder to reverse.

This is where the core mechanism of the book becomes unavoidable. People hold cash because it feels safe. But if costs keep rising while cash remains still, they lose purchasing power. They do not see the loss directly. They feel it. The grocery bill stays high. The repair costs more. The margin disappears. That is how the transfer of wealth continues. The government system does not force participation in the transfer. It creates conditions where most people participate without realizing it. In a fully developed stage of repression, that process stabilizes. Not in a way that restores the old system. In a way that locks in the new one. That is what tomorrow begins to look like.

Not collapse. Narrowing.

CHAPTER 27

When the World Adjusts

How global systems absorb the shift—and send financial pressure back.

If repression deepens inside the United States, it does not stay inside the United States. It moves through the dollar. The dollar is not just domestic currency. It is still central to how much of the world trades, settles, and stores value. Countries still hold U.S. Treasury bonds. Central banks still hold dollar reserves. Financial markets still treat the dollar system as a core reference point. That is why the adjustment spreads. The United States still pays its debts. That part does not change. But what changes is what those dollars are worth when they are returned. If those dollars buy less food, less energy, and less real life than before, then part of the burden has still shifted. The lender is paid. But the value is reduced. This is how repression moves globally, not through default, but through diminished purchasing power inside continued payment.

This matters most in countries tied closely to the dollar. The Kingdom of Saudi Arabia is a clear example. The Saudi riyal is still pegged to the dollar. That creates stability. But it also means the system absorbs dollar weakness. If the dollar loses real purchasing power, the riyal carries that effect. Saudi Arabia does not break the peg immediately. That would introduce instability. Instead, it adjusts through policy, through reserves, and through internal changes. That is how systems respond first. They absorb. Now extend that outward.

Countries like China, Russia, and Brazil have explored ways to reduce dependence on the dollar. This does not create an immediate replacement. There is no sudden moment where one currency replaces another. What happens instead is slower -- more trade happens outside the dollar, payment systems diversify, and alternatives develop at the edges.

The center still holds, but it is less absolute. The question is no longer whether the dollar exists. It is how much of the world continues to rely on it in the same way. If repression continues, that reliance becomes more conditional. Countries still hold Treasuries, but they hedge. They still use dollars, but they test alternatives. They still align, but they diversify. That is how systems change without breaking. Now bring it back to the United States. The country does not lose its position overnight. It still has deep financial markets, a widely used currency, and a global influence. But its position becomes less unquestioned. Instead of being the uncontested center, it becomes the largest player in a system where others are adjusting. That matters because global support has always helped carry the burden. If that support becomes less automatic, internal pressure increases. And that financial pressure does not stay abstract. It moves back into everyday life. It affects cost, stability, and flexibility. And once again, the reader feels it where they always have food, housing, and insurance.

Repression is not just about what happens inside the United States. It is about how the system carries its burden and how much of the world continues to carry it with it.

CHAPTER 28

How to Think About What Comes Next

How to think—not what to buy—when the system keeps moving.

At this point in the book, the reader understands something most people around them may not fully see yet. The system has not reset. The burden has not disappeared. And the pressure is still moving. That realization creates a natural question -- What should someone do with their money?

This book is not here to give financial advice.

It cannot account for someone's personal situation, income, obligations, or risk tolerance. But it can show an example — not of what someone must do, but of how someone might think.

Start with something simple.

Imagine two people. Both feel the financial pressure. Both want to protect themselves. But they respond differently. The first person still has their cash -- but it buys less. The second person may have faced volatility or imperfect decisions -- but they positioned themselves to move with the system instead of standing still against it.

This chapter is not about telling the reader what to buy or sell. It is about helping them understand the environment they are in. Because once the environment is understood, the decisions begin to change naturally.

WHAT REGULAR PEOPLE CAN ACTUALLY DO

The hardest part of a long financial squeeze is feeling like there is nothing to do but watch it happen. There is. Most of the people who came through the 1970s in better shape than their neighbors did not have insider information or unusual luck. They made a small number of practical decisions while there was still time. Those same kinds of decisions are still available today. None of them require a financial background. None of them require a lot of money. And none of them are recommendations — they are descriptions of moves history has shown to be useful when the dollar is quietly losing value.

Lock in fixed costs while you still can. A dollar that buys less next year still pays the same fixed mortgage payment, the same fixed car loan, the same fixed personal loan. Anyone carrying variable-rate debt — credit cards, adjustable-rate mortgages, lines of credit — is exposed every month to whatever the dollar is doing. Anyone with fixed-rate debt is partly protected. Refinancing variable debt into fixed debt, or paying down the variable debt first, is one of the most ordinary decisions a household can make and one of the most powerful in this kind of environment.

Own a little of something real. Throughout history, when paper money has lost value, things people actually use have held value. The reader does not need to become a gold investor to act on this. Buying a small amount of physical gold or silver — even one coin at a time, from a reputable dealer — has historically been enough to give a household a foothold outside the dollar. Owning a home, even a modest one, has historically done the same. So has owning practical things in good condition: a reliable used vehicle, basic tools, a freezer, a generator. These are not investments in the financial sense. They are insulation against a dollar that buys less.

Build a real pantry, not a financial one. In the 1970s, households that bought rice, beans, canned goods, cooking oil, and household basics in bulk effectively locked in last month's prices for next year's meals. The same logic still works. A pantry is not just preparedness — it is a practical hedge against grocery prices that keep rising. The same is true of replacing worn-out essentials before they break: tires, water heaters, eyeglasses, prescriptions filled to the maximum allowed. Each of these is a small purchase made today at today's price instead of next year's.

Reduce what depends on the dollar staying strong. Subscriptions, memberships, financed luxuries, and ongoing service commitments are all promises to keep paying in dollars whose value is moving. Cutting unnecessary recurring expenses is not just budgeting — it is reducing exposure. The dollars saved each month either pay down debt faster, build cash reserves, or fund the small real-asset purchases above.

Make your work harder to replace. In every period of financial pressure, the most secure workers were the ones whose skills were specific, hands-on, and necessary. Electricians, plumbers, mechanics, nurses, welders, HVAC technicians, accountants, and skilled tradespeople kept working when discretionary jobs got cut. The reader does not have to change careers. Adding a practical skill — even slowly, even part-time — is a hedge that no financial product can match. So is keeping professional certifications current, building references, and maintaining the relationships that lead to the next job before the current one ends.

Keep some cash, but know what it is for. Cash loses purchasing power over time, but cash also pays the bills when the unexpected happens. The point is not to hold a lot of cash forever. The point is to hold enough cash to avoid being forced to sell something — a car, a home, a long-held asset — at the worst possible moment. History shows that the people who suffered most in periods like this were usually the ones who had to make a desperate sale at a bad price. A modest cash cushion prevents that.

Talk to a real professional before doing anything large. Everything above is small, ordinary, and within reach of a normal household. Anything bigger — buying property, making a major investment, restructuring retirement accounts, selling a business — deserves a conversation with a licensed financial advisor, a tax professional, or an attorney who knows the reader's specific situation. This book cannot give that advice. The professionals the reader hires can.

The point is not to predict the future. The point is to stop waiting for the old world to come back, and to start making the small, ordinary decisions that history has shown make a real difference when the dollar is quietly losing ground. The final decision the reader faces is simple -- do they remain in the conditions the system creates, or do they begin thinking differently because they now see them? That is the only real choice this book offers.

CLOSING

Clarity over prediction.

The financial system does not end. It shifts. The question is not whether it survives, but rather what it becomes and who continues to absorb the cost.

This book was not written to predict the future. It was written to make the present readable. Because once the pattern becomes visible, what once felt random begins to feel connected. The pressure no longer feels like a personal failure. It feels like what it is -- a structural shift moving through the government system, through the dollar, through global alignment, and through everyday life.

The reader cannot control the financial system, but they can control their clarity. And once they see it, they no longer wait for the old world to return. Instead, they begin preparing for the world they are actually living in.

That is the clarity this book offers.

ACKNOWLEDGMENTS

To everyone who has felt the squeeze without being given the language to explain it — your experience is real, and it deserves clarity.

To the readers who kept asking why everything still feels off — your questions shaped this book.

To those who continue trying to build stability in an unstable environment — your persistence is the quiet strength behind every chapter.

NOTES

This book draws on public-record sources: official government documents, agency data, and major news coverage from outlets including Reuters, the Associated Press, the Wall Street Journal, NPR, CNN, Bloomberg, and others. The citations below identify the primary sources for the specific factual claims made in each chapter. URLs are provided for the most direct reference where available.

INTRODUCTION

General macroeconomic context throughout the book draws on Federal Reserve Economic Data (FRED) at fred.stlouisfed.org, International Monetary Fund World Economic Outlook publications at imf.org, and U.S. Treasury debt statistics at treasurydirect.gov.

CHAPTER 3

Executive Order 14159, "Protecting the American People Against Invasion," signed January 20, 2025. Federal Register, 90 FR 8443 (January 29, 2025). Presidential Proclamation 10888, "Guaranteeing the States Protection Against Invasion," January 20, 2025. Federal Register, 90 FR 8333. Executive Order 14165, "Securing Our Borders," January 20, 2025. Full text of all three is available at federalregister.gov.

CHAPTER 4

White House Fact Sheet, "President Donald J. Trump Imposes Tariffs on Imports from Canada, Mexico and China," February 1, 2025. The 25% tariffs on most goods from Mexico and Canada took effect March 4, 2025; selective USMCA carve-outs were issued

March 6, 2025. On May 28, 2025, the U.S. Court of International Trade ruled the IEEPA-based tariffs exceeded executive authority; on February 20, 2026, the U.S. Supreme Court affirmed that the legal basis for most of these tariffs was invalid.

CHAPTER 6

Federal civilian workforce data: U.S. Office of Personnel Management Federal Workforce Data tools at opm.gov. Pew Research Center, "Federal workforce shrank 10% in Trump's first year back in office," March 13, 2026. Boston Globe analysis of OPM data, February 26, 2026 (approximately 10% decline). Federal News Network analysis of OPM data, January 2026 (13.7% decline measured against the September 2024 baseline). U.S. Bureau of Labor Statistics employment data via FRED. See https://www.pewresearch.org/short-reads/2026/03/13/federal-workforce-shrank-10-in-trumps-first-year-back-in-office/

CHAPTER 7

Congressional Research Service Report R45281, "Iran Conflict and the Strait of Hormuz: Impacts on Oil, Gas, and Other Commodities," March 2026. U.S.–Israel air operations against Iran began February 28, 2026; Iran declared the Strait of Hormuz closed on March 4, 2026; a ceasefire was announced April 8, 2026, though shipping volumes remained well below pre-war levels. Brent crude prices rose 10–13% in early March 2026 trading and surged past $120 per barrel by mid-March, prompting the International Energy Agency to describe the event as the largest supply shock in the history of the global oil market. International Monetary Fund Regional Economic Outlook for the Middle East and Central Asia, imf.org. See https://www.congress.gov/crs_external_products/R/PDF/R45281/R45281.6.pdf last visited on 20 April 2026.

CHAPTER 8

Executive Order 14160 of January 20, 2025, addressing birthright citizenship. Trump v. Barbara, oral argument before the Supreme Court of the United States, April 1, 2026; decision pending as of publication. Contemporaneous coverage: SCOTUSblog, NPR, CNN, and the Associated Press, all dated April 1, 2026. See https://www.govinfo.gov/content/pkg/DCPD-202500127/pdf/DCPD-202500127.pdf last visited on 20 April 2026.

CHAPTER 11

Executive Order 14178, "Strengthening American Leadership in Digital Financial Technology," signed January 23, 2025. White House Fact Sheet, January 24, 2025. The President's Working Group on Digital Asset Markets released its report July 31, 2025. The GENIUS Act, establishing a federal regulatory framework for stablecoins, was signed into law July 18, 2025. See https://www.govinfo.gov/content/pkg/DCPD-202500169/pdf/DCPD-202500169.pdf last visited on 20 April 2026.

CHAPTER 28

Historical references to the 1970s draw on Federal Reserve History essays at federalreservehistory.org ("The Great Inflation," "Nixon Ends Convertibility"), Bureau of Labor Statistics CPI data, and standard reference works on the period. None of the chapter constitutes financial, legal, or tax advice; all readers are encouraged to consult licensed professionals about their specific situations. See, e.g., https://www.federalreservehistory.org/essays/great-inflation last visited on 20 April 2026.

GENERAL DATA SOURCES

Consumer prices, employment, and household income: U.S. Bureau of Labor Statistics, bls.gov. Treasury debt, deficit, and federal budget data: U.S. Department of the Treasury, treasurydirect.gov, and the Congressional Budget Office, cbo.gov. International economic data: International Monetary Fund World Economic Outlook, imf.org. Federal Reserve policy actions and market data: Federal Reserve Board, federalreserve.gov.

All interpretations, framing, and narrative structure are the author's own.

GLOSSARY

Short, clear definitions for readers with little or no economics background.

Purchasing power — How much real life your money can buy — food, housing, energy, services.

Liquidity — How easily money moves through the system. High liquidity supports markets even when life feels tight.

Financial Rails — The hidden infrastructure that moves money — bank networks, settlement systems, payment pathways.

Settlement — The moment a payment becomes final. Faster settlement reduces friction and risk.

Repression — A system where the government avoids a clean reset by spreading the burden quietly through everyday life.

Nominal Value — The number printed on money or shown in an account — not what it can actually buy.

Real Value — What your money can buy in the real world.

Treasury Bonds / Notes — Loans to the U.S. government. They can repay in full while still losing purchasing power if the dollar weakens.

Pegged Currency — A currency tied to another (like the Saudi riyal to the U.S. dollar). Stability comes with shared pressure.

Utility Crypto — Digital systems designed to move value efficiently — not speculation, but infrastructure.

ABOUT THE AUTHOR

André J. Porter is a legal professional and nonfiction author who studies how financial systems absorb pressure and how policy decisions move through everyday life. His work focuses on explaining structural forces in clear, accessible language for general readers. He writes through his imprint, Quiet Mechanics Press.

www.ingramcontent.com/pod-product-compliance
Lightning Source LLC
LaVergne TN
LVHW090537110826
845146LV00003B/1143
* 9 7 9 8 9 9 5 8 3 1 6 0 0 *